How To Really Save Our Children

How To Really Save Our Children

LINDA LORRAINE JAMES

HOW TO REALLY SAVE OUR CHILDREN

iUniverse books may be ordered through booksellers or by contacting:

iUniverse
1663 Liberty Drive
Bloomington, IN 47403
www.iuniverse.com
844-349-9409

ISBN: 978-1-6632-3915-0 (sc)
ISBN: 978-1-6632-3914-3 (e)

Library of Congress Control Number: 2022907876

Print information available on the last page.

iUniverse rev. date: 06/24/2022

Contents

Acknowledgments

A heartfelt sincere thanks is mine to express first of all to my husband, who is also my pastor, Bishop Vernon L. James of the Johnson Street Christ Holy Sanctified Church and first vice president of the Christ Holy Sanctified Churches of America Inc. Thank you for your love and devotion to God and our marriage. June 25, 2021 marks our fiftieth year of marriage. All the praise belongs to God for blessing our love.

To my children Vernon II, Verlondra, Reuben, and Lamega: my gratitude and love run deep as the oceans for you. I offer special tribute to my first-born son, Vernon II, who passed away in 1999; he is my inspiration to complete this book. Verlondra and Reuben, you are my pride and joy, as you have been the greatest supporters a mother could have. My children have blessed me and encouraged me to journey on. I love you and thank you for loving me.

Special thanks to my mother, Ruby Willams, who taught me how to be that special daughter and to continue keep listening to and looking to God. My heart is truly grateful for Mary Katherine and Willie James, otherwise known as Ma and Dad! They have been two solid rocks throughout my life. Thanks also to my big brother Marvin and my little brother Dwyane, both of whom I dearly love. God has smiled on us in countless and amazing ways. Dwyane has passed on, but his love lives on in an unending story for our family.

To my church family and all the wonderful members who display their love so remarkably and go above and beyond in their support of the pastor, wife, and first family: we are so elated to be blessed and encouraged by you.

My spiritual wall of fame is galvanized by the names of the great people who poured into my life, in their own unique ways of encouragement.

Ecclesiastes 3:11, he has made everything beautiful in its time. For this I am grateful.

Introduction

Have you met that person that can make you smile at your lowest?
That can make you believe the unbelievable?
One whose words pierce not only your heart,
but can penetrate your soul.
Someone who cares so much, loves so much, and trusts so much.
Someone who is on your side, no matter what the
odds. We have ... and that someone is you.
—Written by my son Reuben to "Mama"

It is now time to complete the writing of my journey through my book, *How to Really Save Our Children*.

Thank God for our marriage and our walk with God together. We are blessed to be proud parents of three children, Vernon II, Verlondra, and Reuben. Our son Vernon II, affectionately known as "Tiger," is my inspiration for writing this book. Tiger's life tragically ended at the age of twenty-six. I will share his life in greater detail as I continue my writing of this book. I must say, the impact of his life and love still lives on in the hearts of our family.

Then there is my daughter Verlondra. Her dad calls her Angel, and that name describes exactly who she is. Verlondra is a rare jewel in our family, priceless and beautiful inside and out. I love her beyond measures for who she is and all that she contributes in our family. She is our true-to-life guardian angel. My daughter has sacrificed greatly as she and my son Reuben shared in the life of our granddaughter Briana. It's like she is Briana's guardian angel mama. Verlondra is that angel, hovering over with outstretched wings, that keeps on protecting. It's as if she is an auntie who has an inspiring gift of super powers. She can leap into action at a moment's notice. It was no ordinary venture as Verlondra persevered to be part of Briana's journey for the best quality of normalcy in life. She was there through many tears of joy and many tears of pain. During countless doctor visits for Briana, she was there. Even the times I couldn't press on, she took charge. She would wheel Briana on to the van, take her to her appointments, and call me if the doctor had any questions that required my attention. She did it all, and she did it with excellence. Sometimes she would take Briana's friends with her, just to make Briana happy and keep her smiling. It made therapy for Briana worth it all to be surrounded by those who loved and motivated her. I can just imagine them saying, "Come on Bri, you can do it," and Bri did it with a smile.

To embrace this nurturing is amazing. Verlondra is my one and only phenomenal daughter. In spite of her pain, she loved and cared for someone in even greater pain.

Verlondra is a great source of strength for our family. Her love remains unwavering for the family. She put us all first because she cared. This was quite a load, and she carried it like Wonder Woman.

God has blessed me with such an abundance of love and grateful appreciation for my daughter. With the greatest love as her mother, I celebrate Verlondra for the angel that she is. My daughter has prevailed through many circumstances concerning our family. This was not an easy journey, and I know this was not the dream she had for herself. Thank God for her spirit, strength, and generosity that keep on sustaining. She has gone above and beyond. Verlondra is my princess daughter, loved and cherished in my heart. I have been blessed because of her example of love and dedication to family. Her dream and plans were halted when her brother Tiger was killed. The road came to a dead end. Suddenly, there was another uncharted territory.

Without reservation, you consider the needs of those you hold dearest in your life. In no way was it easy, but Verlondra trusted her heart and allowed it to guide. Briana needed us, and that was reason enough to be there for her. Briana was the first-born daughter of her first-born brother. There was no idea of all that would transpire in the next twenty plus years. What a long haul of a journey about to take place. This long haul changed the direction of our family unit. Verlondra was in it to win, and she rose to the challenge.

Every young girl dreams of how their lives will evolve in their future. They have dreams of going away to college, followed by that perfect job, the perfect mate, and ultimately the picture-perfect family.

In quite an unexpected turn of life and love, another season occurred. Her life was turned upside down and went totally off the grid.

We all became trailblazers embarking on new and unfamiliar horizons and territories.

My youngest son, Reuben, is the epitome of joy that keeps on spreading. He too, was put in this position. You have to understand he is truly a best friend to his sister and a blessing to our family. Reuben simply loves life and people. It takes very little to sustain his happiness. Jeremiah 17:17 says, but blessed is the one who trusts in the Lord, whose confidence is in Him. There is such adoration and appreciation just being around Reuben. He will turn anything into a song of extreme happiness. He's the type who eases on down the yellow brick road. There is such a heartfelt passion about him.

It is evident that there is an anointed connection through his writing and singing. God ministers the words to sing to him followed by the rhythm and beat. He then hears the song in his heart. Reuben can sing the perfect combination of pitch and rhythm that ushers in the spirit of praise and worship.

This connection came at a very low time in life during the death of his brother, Tiger. He began to listen to songs by the iconic Fred Hammond that would minister to his periods of grief. In fact, it enabled him to cope with his loss. He not only coped, but greatly expressed himself through writing songs and singing under the anointing. This was before he even realized his gift of singing and writing songs.

In times of grief, you experience hurt, pain, and anger. In those times of not knowing the answer, you allow the Holy Spirit to remind you of whose you are. We realize God won't put more on you than you can bear. At times, we may find ourselves overtaken with life's experiences on this journey. God's grace and mercy is continuously there to love and sustain us through all healing processes.

Reuben has a compassion for loving people. He is always laughing and making life, our life fun. He allowed the real power that strengthens him to sustain him in this dark hour.

My son makes you feel important and loved. You see it in his love for his wife, Lamega, and his girls Morgan, Addison, and Rhilee. It is expressed in the meaningful little things he does. Reuben tickles me until I laugh uncontrollably, just to make me feel my best. You sense it in his compassion for his sister, who calls him her best friend. He offers her that listening ear whenever she needs it. You sense it in the way he attends to the instruction of his father, even though he too is a father. He can be the calming effect in difficult situations.

As small children, Reuben and Verlondra were typical siblings who had the task of being subjected to the authority of their big brother, Tiger, who would attempt to be the big brother and boss his younger siblings. Verlondra, being the middle child and the only girl, would hold her own, but Reuben had to defend his title as little brother.

When I speak of my children, many thoughts overflow and I bounce back and forth with inspiration.

My children continuously express their love through their support of the endeavors God has placed in my heart. It takes this united effort to succeed in the vision God has placed in the family. Their gifts, talents and ministry are part of our school's campaign, "Fort Worth Save Our Children," which deserves the credit and holds the reason behind *How to Really Save Our Children.*

Then there's my mother dear:
a tribute to a very special lady

As her only daughter, I am honored to give tribute to my precious mother. Her name is Ruby. She has always encouraged me. When I was a child, she would call me Miss Prissy, and still speaks about how prissy I was. To me she is Madea and taught me to be a lady, confident in who I was. It didn't matter what the other little girls did, I knew I had best stand apart from trouble. Somehow, trouble was always there, giving me a run for my money. I ran as hard and as fast as I could. My mother continues to remind me of how proud she is of our family. She speaks often of how God blessed our marriage these many years.

Madea is elegant, refined, and graceful. She has always aspired to be the best at what she does. She has always desired to motivate others to improve themselves. Early on in her adult life, she enrolled in cosmetology school and learned the skills of doing hair and all that comes with it.

Upon completion of cosmetology school, she worked in white salons. In so doing, Madea made many Caucasian friendships working in cosmetology. Everybody loved her. Through these many friendships, Madea would also take on the task of decorating and cleaning her client's homes. She would make outstanding hors d'oeuvres and finger foods and arrange them beautifully on platters. Everyone loved all this talent my mom had. Her gift made room for her. As time progressed, she worked for one family until she retired. It was like her own family. She worked in their home as well as at their various businesses. She used this gift at home and at church. She would have our church looking so beautiful at all times. The arrangement of plants and tables and furniture in various locations really beautified the church. Madea took her time and thought things through. Just to see her take notes as she visualized what she wanted and then to see the finished product resulted in everyone's awe and amazement.

My mom is a beautiful woman, and she carries herself with grace and elegance. As a child, when she would visit my school, I would be so proud to say she was my mom. The kids would say she was pretty and then ask why she was so much more light-skinned than I was. I would always say I stayed in the sun too much. I had no clue as to the answer to this question.

In school I was pretty much average and made good grades. I was never that over-the-top honor student, but I was smart and could hold my own. During my senior year in high school, I was in distributive education and worked a job part-time. By this time my interest in extracurricular activities at school was at a new low. My class was in a new school building and even had our graduation there.

The fall after graduation, I went off to college about fifty miles away from home. It was a small Christian-based Assemblies of God College. My mom was my support system, along with student loans that had to be repaid. These loans eventually became mine to repay. At the time, however, I had no idea of the expense and no knowledge of what paying for your education really meant. The truth of the matter was, I could not afford it. All I knew was that I was in college.

I wasn't used to living away from home and certainly not in a dorm. It was basically a hotel, and my roommate and I occupied a bedroom. We even had to share the dorm showers. We would carry our grooming accessories and make our way down the hallway to the accommodations for college girls. My roommate and I were the only blacks living in the dorm at the predominantly white college in this small town. This unfamiliar experience and environment were totally outside my element. College life became a tremendous adjustment for me and my roommate. We did it, though. I completed two years and received my associate degree in business. I was then more than ready to return home to be with my mom. I worked and lived at home until I got married.

In many ways, from day one Madea had definitely been there to help with our children, our home, and our church. She adds a touch of class to what she does, from decorating spaces to speaking on the scriptures. My mom is very soft-spoken and can accomplish most anything she visualizes in decorating.

Finally, I give homage and tribute to Briana, our first of six granddaughters. She is special and incredible to our family. God has honored and allowed us to love and care for her. Briana is our gift in such a special capacity. During infancy, she was diagnosed with cerebral palsy. Our family is blessed to be her caregivers, and she is with us 24/7. Much of how to really save our children comes from a lifetime with Briana. The stage has been set for this miraculous journey.

I could go on and on about the many family members and friends who have played a major part in bringing life to my book. My purpose is that everyone who reads it will be touched by the awesomeness of what God can do in the life of someone like me. I am inspired to write and share what God has done in my life. God can and does use ordinary people from simple backgrounds and fills them with purpose. God has given me such purpose for this season in life. It has been my personal struggle in completing this project. For years, I have allowed time and circumstances to block and delay my progress. I have been guilty as charged for making excuses and placing on hold the writing of *How to Really Save Our Children*. It's a new dawn for me, and I thank God that the steps of a man are established by the Lord. It is an honor to now take advantage of this great opportunity to write my heart's inspiration.

It has been part of my destiny and in my heart to write this book. My endeavor of making this book a reality has always dominated my spirit. In my procrastination and delaying to write this book, it seemed as if I was always waiting for a better season or a better time. I even thought I was waiting on a deeper conviction before I could write.

With all that said, I am ready to share in my heart's desire to impact the lives of our young people. Being optimistic and positive about my life's journey concerning our children, I am sharing from my innermost being and from my heart, the cause of my journey and intentions to make a difference. Every aspect from changing diapers to teaching in this ministry of saving our children has proven to be a gift and proclamation from God.

It all started with the inspiring dream of one day becoming a teacher. To what extent I would do this was a dream within itself. I thought maybe I would start with small beginnings and then conquer the world with the plan of how to really save our children. My journey needed a starting point and a plan of navigation. Proverbs 3:36 KJV: "In all thy ways acknowledge Him and He shall direct thy paths." Here it is, as I am blessed to put this journey to pen and paper. It is to my delight and pleasure to share in my journey of hope and love for our children. Although I am sharing this phase of book writing, there still remains a greater destination to be accomplished on my life's amazing journey.

It is my honor to first and foremost express my gratefulness to God for allowing me, the little girl who moved from the little town of Kerens with her mother and brother and relocated to the north side of Fort Worth—there to stay with my mom's sister, affectionately known as "Aunt Sugar," and her husband, "Uncle Shot." After a brief stay with them, we moved to the Stop Six Projects. All these changes were part of the journey in my life, a life that was influenced by the power of love.

Without a doubt God inspired me in his infinite power to become part of many lives.

Without our families and parents seeking a safe place for their babies, and then entrusting Save Our Children day care and learning center to be that safe place, there would be no Sister Linda with a journey to share. My desire is to share with our worldwide community the making of my dream. Like in any successful endeavor, one may want to have accomplished even more. Because of that same desire, I am determined to be an inspiration. My journey has been illuminating, because God has placed this desire in me. The sooner we allow our faith to line up with our purpose, the sooner we maximize our potential and even beyond that. To God be the glory for inspiring me to write my story.

The power of the influence upon my life from a child afforded me the opportunity to make a difference in the precious lives of many children in such a significant way.

In the Bible, in the book of Jeremiah 20:11, it reads: "for I know the thoughts that I think toward you saith the Lord, thoughts of peace, and not evil, to give you an expected end." I know God has custom designed His plans for me to write. I pray this book will serve as an inspiration because of the many lives I have been blessed to share in. God has blessed me to contribute to the wholeness of our young people. Honors to the many teachers and caregivers that gave and yet give of themselves. It definitely was not a get rich quick job, but one of dedication to the purpose.

To all the many influential role models in my life: we have a great task in helping to shape the lives of our little ones. Matthew 19:14–15 reads in the application study bible: "Let the children come to me. Don't stop them. For the kingdom of heaven belongs to such as these," and Jesus put his hands on their heads and blessed them before He left. I am such as one of these children. Being blessed by the hand of God, I dedicate my life to the God of my salvation.

CHAPTER 1

Write the Vision …
Heart, Soul, and Mind

In the Bible, in Habakkuk 2, it tells us about writing the vision and making it plain that they may run and not faint. For the vision is only for a while, it will speak and not lie.

Early in life I envisioned becoming a teacher. This was evident even in my preference of playtime with my childhood friends. As we played "school," this environment consisted of the roles of student and teacher. My only option was to be the teacher exclusively, or I would not participate. In fact, whatever games we played, I had to be the leader, the one in charge of giving directions.

There was a candid quality of doing things my own way that pushed me. Improvising as I proceeded was to be a trailblazer, so to speak. Perfect timing was a top priority in compelling me to press forward.

I accepted Christ at an early age, and the church became the most important thing to me. All my friends were at the church. Everything I was inspired to do was because of accepting Christ in my life. I loved the Lord and wanted to be of service and in His will.

My spiritual connection with my church family allowed for growth in my love for God and my relationship with Him. I felt my greatest joy when I was with my church family and friends. With my praying and seeking God, I wanted more of this spiritual experience and being committed to God. I was grateful for the Bible teaching found in Acts 16:31, where it says, believe on the Lord Jesus Christ and thou shalt be saved. Through the mentoring of the seasoned women of the church, I built on that sure foundation of loving trust in sound counsel. Colossians 3:23 says, whoever walks with the wise becomes wise. The church became a safe refuge far beyond my expectations. The plan of salvation fully persuaded me to journey on.

Everything started when the child within me desired to be changed into the woman God destined for the journey of how to really save our children. First and foremost, I had to be saved myself. Through many intimate prayerful conversations with God, I found encouragement to continue moving forward in this season.

To my amazement, I begin to discover inward beauty and the needs of the children of our community. These children, in spite of who they were or where they lived, needed to be confident with who they were journeying to become. Already being in the minority, an additional boost in self-worth and self-esteem could only serve as a bonus.

I had to work hard at self-approval. There was no silver spoon for me to boast about.

I had to work at being happy with myself. There were personal issues with my ears sticking out and my short, cotton soft, and thin hair. Actually, I dealt with these issues for years, and still do. I just know a better means to handle it, so I do what I do. Self- confidence is something I work at. My friends thought I was naturally unhesitating in my personally, but I have always pushed myself to overcome, to be my best, to dress my best, and control as many situations as I could. Actually, I still battle with this internal warfare, but I was born to win. It is very personal to me, and I would rather not take on the task of convincing anyone else otherwise. The response is always, "Yeah, right!" I realize what the Lord has done, so I walk in my "Yeah, right blessing!

As a young lady, I was petite, dainty, and ladylike, which is something my mom insisted on. Parental controls were a must for me. Although we lived in the projects and were subject to undesirable lifestyles, I was not to be a product of that environment. How I carried myself was most important to me. Such innocence involved the help of decent neighbors who cared about us children and watched out for us. They also had children they wanted protected from the ways of the hood and the streets. These were Christian parents that invited their neighbors and children to church. There were several churches in the vicinity, so you had your choice.

There were times I would stray away from the good path and journey a little off course. I loved music and the many singers in '60s era. This little girl was a dancing machine, and dancing was my forte'. I would watch these dancing shows, "Teenage Downbeat and American Bandstand." After school, I had my friends over, and we would dance until it was time for my mom and stepdad to come home. They would get off the city bus, and I could see them coming in the distance. With time to clear them out, I would rush my friends out of the back door. Low and behold, one day my mom caught them going out the back door. Needless to say, I had to revise that plan and revise it in a hurry. The rod of correction found itself searching for and finding me.

My mom was invited to go to a church in the community by friends she had met in the projects. We went, and what did she do that for? It was not a church, but it was a neighborhood mission. Its leader was a little missionary lady who would gather the neighbor kids along with her two boys and teach the Word of God. Afterwards, we had refreshments. This would encourage a lot of us project kids to attend. Her sole purpose and intentions were to church us little kids and our families. She fed us, preached to us, and then came the focal point of praying for us. I could not say how sincere my friends were, but they seemed as though they were. Knowing I wasn't, it all appeared strange to me. I would just look at my friends. The more she prayed with my friends, the more they would begin to seek the spirit of God. Unfamiliar with all that crying out and praying to God, I was perplexed.

When I saw my good friend fall out in the spirit, I was pondering, thinking just maybe this was real. Amid her praying and seeking God, she was slain in the power of the Holy Ghost. She was real this time. I wanted to feel what she felt. I didn't know what it was, but I wanted it too. I didn't know what I was expecting to happen. I assumed on my own that in order to get the spirit like my friends, I would have to purge myself of all the worldly dancing I loved to do. Again, I figured what better way to display my dancing ability one last time. It would serve as my sacrificial repentance. Through this ignorance, I grabbed hands with the missionary who was praying, and I began to dance. Being quite determined, I did the mash potato, the twist, the calypso, the jerk; you name the dance, I did it in that prayer meeting. Needless to say, my friends laughed at me and said I was just dancing. As I cried out, I too began to feel the presence of the Lord. The spirit did minister to me. As a result of this neighborhood prayer mission, I wanted even more of this newly found presence of the spirit of the Lord. I wanted to experience the greater of God's spirit in my heart.

CHAPTER 2

Follow Your Dream of a Lifetime

The journey of a lifetime was in my grasp, but I had to stay the course. To follow the dream and make the change, I had to dwell in the secret place of the Most High. Finding solutions to these changes had to be resolved. The future of these changes is included in the dream. Doing my best for God included following His plan. This transformation involved a renewing of my passion for the journey without compromising the dream.

At an early age I began to understand that God has a destiny for His people. He brings us from one season to another, as well as destination to destination. Having said this, I was on a journey of change, a change that was faithfully declared. I didn't see the destination, but that's where faith and trust triumphs in my journey.

It was my season, and a change of course was destined. It would be of the utmost importance to shift from one place in life to another.

May I say, I may not see all of where God is taking me, but great is His faithfulness.

Hebrews 11:1 says faith is being sure of what we hope for and certain of what we do not see ... and without faith it is impossible to please God, because anyone who come to Him must believe that He exists; and He rewards those who diligently seek Him. I believed God was directing me on the plans to impact the lives of the children and families I would encounter with "Save Our Children," my new assignment. As God began to map plans, I began to feel the changes in my heart. There was a shifting and drive to stay the course. I had to follow step by step. Following God was my confident obligation. Even in the times I became side-tracked, the Lord became my strength and my defense.

In my endeavor to trust God to teach me the experiences of how to really save our children, I had to develop the mind of Christ. The scripture says in Philippians 2:5, let this mind be in you that was also in Christ Jesus. And be not conformed to this world, but be ye transformed by the renewing of your mind, that you may prove what is that good and acceptable and perfect will of God.

I couldn't just go around in circles. That would get me nowhere. Neither could I just keep straight, because life has turns and U-turns. We may have to double back, or even tread a bridge over troubled waters. Then there is the possibility we may have to switch to another highway in life. While on this highway, we often experience long stretches of nothing. Just stay the course. We may have to refuel, or stop and rest. Just know that change is part of the plan. Don't get confused when we don't see the destination up the road; just follow the plan God has mapped out for our lives. It may seem like we ought to go another direction; just stay the course. Rest when you should and refuel as often as necessary; it's all part of the plan. You will arrive at each and every destination.

As I journeyed this course of how to really save our children, I traveled on what I felt was not the right road. However, I had to stay the course and continue making plans to reach my destination.

As I reference the journey of saving our children, I must continue my focus. There was this inner drive to take some certain routes, and one proved to be a course that led to refueling. This allowed me to stay the course. My refueling place in life sometimes took years. One of these refuelings in my life lasted over fourteen years. I just had to wait until my tank was full, so that I could continue.

As I navigated through my spiritual journey of saving our children, I had to trust God and keep the faith.

It is with loving anticipated pleasure that I share from the heart of Sister Linda.

CHAPTER 3

Where Do I Begin?

We have all watched movies that begin at the end of the story, then flash back to someone telling how it all started, and then lead up to the now. I am sure you get my drift. Well, just a warning, because this is how my journey will flow. My numerous inspirations, hurts, pains, disappointments, and joys have rendered me the opportunity to share this journey of *How to Really Save Our Children*. These experiences have positioned me for such a time as this. There is a place in my heart to share the truth of my story, my journey.

My husband Vernon and I own and operate Fort Worth Save Our Children, a day care and private school. We initially served infants through seventh grade. At one point we served through ninth grade. It has been an honor and blessing to have experienced this opportunity to share in the lives of the many infants, students and their families.

As I began to seek God and grow in faith and obedience to God, as I seek more divine guidance, it has led me to concentrate on my innate qualities. It became essential to explore my desire to journal my life. As this desire deepened, I listened to hear the voice of God. The scripture reminds me that faith comes by hearing and hearing by the word of God. It was to my advantage to respond to that voice and not neglect this moment.

"How to save really save our children" is a catchy title that attempts to stir and attract the interest and attention of the reader. The title insinuates the possibility of being a manual with precise and straightforward directions to rescue our children from dangers encountered in life.

In essence, the title stems from my love for God and the innocence of children. Thus evolved my desire to help our children become complete and confident in their quest for the best life. Sharing in this manner was my personal approach to assure success and greatness in God.

My life has included experiences of both joys and pains. Being secure in the loving arms of God sustains me through difficulty. My faith in God keeps me from allowing life's disappointments to defeat me. Whenever life throws unexpected curves intended to strike me out, God is there guiding every move. His love guarantees the victory. Acts 8:37 reminds us that in all these things we are more than conquerors through Him who loves us.

Keep in mind the title of my book is, *How to Really Save Our Children*, but in essence the focus is about me, Sis. Linda, as I define my journey: a woman who loves everything associated with service to God. This love sustains me and brings purpose, peace, and patience to my life.

I am not a professional writer by trade, but by life's experiences. I have titles and accolades that are associated with what I do and who I am in life, but my safe place name is just Sis. Linda. This journey has presented me countless experiences of love, joy, peace, hurt, anger, failures, success, misfortunes, and disappointments as I remained surrounded in the loving the arms of God. In this place I feel safe, saved, and protected. This is the place where God ministers to the child within.

I find myself inspired when I realize it's all about the power of this love manifested in my life because of God and in spite all else.

This manifestation causes me to realize what it takes to really save our children, what it takes to save the child within us. We are continually reassured by our heavenly Father and the spirit He so freely gives.

Our school, Fort Worth Save Our Children, started as a dream. I humbly confess my gratitude to the Lord that it is and has remained a reality for more than thirty-five blessed years.

Years ago, one of our parents at Save Our Children adopted a slogan and began to lovingly refers to our school as the "best kept secret in Fort Worth." The secret began to spread by word of mouth, and the vision remain reality.

CHAPTER 4

Make Plans to Change

The passion to teach and share with children started early in life. As a child when playing, whatever the game, I had to be the mama, the boss, or the teacher. I would choose to be in control and determine how the game was played.

Our school started as a dream and a vision as well. I still dream and visualize the greater potential for Save Our Children. God has graced us to be an avenue of inspiration and aspiration in the lives of the families and children associated with our school.

To advance in our journey of life, we have to do things differently to accomplish change, so we make plans to do so. We come to realize the importance of our purpose. The question is, why do I do what I do?

As we relate to the seasons of the year changing, so do the seasons of our fulfilling our destiny evolve. God carries us from season to season and expectation to expectation. We don't see the surface of each road before we get to it, but with our measure of faith, we follow and trust the GPA that God divinely supplied us. God has ordained our lives, and by faith we reach each destination. The scripture in the book of Hebrews 11 tells us that faith is the substance of things hoped for and the evidence of things not seen.

So, if we keep the faith and believe our destination is up the road, then like the car's navigation system, we just follow the course. This includes right turns, left turns, and even traveling straight stretches for miles and miles on many given destinations.

Many times, on this journey of saving our children, I have found myself off course, trying to maneuver a short cut. These situations require a rerouting to get back on course. This caused me to reroute, U-turn, double back to the bridge, switch back to the main highway, and again follow the course. The guarantee to reaching destiny is to stay the course as we follow God's directions.

As we navigate our spiritual journey of saving our children, this same concept proves to be a truth. We must continue trusting God.

Once again, I reflect back to one very dear to my heart. As an adult, a child's life changes as they encounter and make their own choices. Being God-loving parents, you nourish your child and raise them with godly principles in the home, you take them to church, and endeavor to put them in a Christian education environment to counter negative influences of the enemy. We go the distance, and even after all this, there comes the time when their choices are not advised by parental discretion.

It's easy to talk about our first son and how do we all loved him. However, when I write about him, this heartfelt presence of his love comes over me, and I find it difficult to continue without my emotions going to maximum speed. I usually end up stopping at these points in my writing and tend to grieve our loss. But this time I am pressing on, heart aching and all, because I want to complete my assignment to write about my journey and my love for my children.

Vernon II (Tiger) is our first child, and there are so many first-time experiences concerning him. We learned a lot together as first-time parents with a busy boy who was a handful. We knew a lot more when Verlondra and Reuben arrived.

Verlondra often told me that Tiger made it tough for her and

Reuben. Anytime I could enhance their obedience, they say, I did so. I love them deeply, and I thank God for our three children, Vernon, Verlondra, and Reuben. Our only daughter and youngest son are so protective and loving of their parents' hearts. They go above and beyond to help our family endeavors in the home, church, and the school, Fort Worth Save Our Children.

For over thirty-five years now, my husband Vernon and I have owned and operated Fort Worth Save Our Children Day Care and Learning Center. Our students have ranged from infants to as high as ninth grade. At this time of writing, we are at the fifth grade level. Verlondra and Reuben are yet devoted to the school ministry with us. We also have other family members who have contributed greatly to the success of the school. It is a family affair because of the love and support of so many. Appreciation and love go to each of them. We have definitely been very blessed by influential people with the means to pour into Fort Worth Save Our Children. We are blessed and thankful to God for our longevity. Many students and families have graced us with the opportunity to teach and impact their lives in a positive way.

My heart mind and soul are determined to share my story about this awesome journey I am yet on and the power of God to direct and order my footsteps, steps that I continue to make with God as my source and guide. I am thankful and grateful for the opportunity to do my share. I sincerely know I am fulfilling my purpose in life because of the Almighty God. It has been and still is an incredible journey. It is a God-ordained opportunity to be involved in this awesome responsibility of shaping the lives of our children. It is small in comparisons to so many other great Christians schools and institutions of learning. Even as small as we are, we have done what we were organized to do. Because we care, we give our best to save our children. In turn, God has blessed us to find favor and love from others who cared enough to help and become our friends.

As in the words of the song, "What do you do when you've done all you can?" The answer is you just stand and endure. It goes on to say God has a purpose, and God has a plan. I am here to say the plan of God unfolds through our faithfulness and obedience to Him.

CHAPTER 5

Life Is What It Is

Growing up, we often dream and talk about how our adult lives will be. For some reason, I had this big fantasy of being this corporate secretary who would move through the ranks and become the executive director of the whole operation, whatever all that meant to me at that time.

Once I did work in the corporate world, I quickly realized this was not my calling. I was there for a nearly fifteen-year season, but my heart was elsewhere. In this season of my life, I learned more and more about dealing with all types of people from all walks of life, from the meek and lowly to the high and mighty. My experiences were preparing me for what I was to become.

While desiring the reality of this dream of executive secretary and CEO of my own company, little did I know I was walking on that path destined for me.

There were many things I learned working in the corporate world. The knowledge I gained served only to prepare me for where God would establish me. It is a journey that is near and dear to my heart. God has blessed us to pour into the lives of children and their families.

It is what it is. By this I mean, this is purpose at its finest.

Without a doubt it is a dream and vision being fulfilled. Life at Save Our Children has created amazing relationships and life-changing experiences.

"Oh, that we may know the Lord! Let us press on to know Him. He will respond to us as surely as the rising of the dawn or the coming of rains in the early spring." (Hosea 6:3 NLT)

I was feeling the urgency of the spirit to move into the next phase of God's plan. I was living during a time in my life when finances were aligning with the lifestyle I wanted at this time. My life allowed me to be in a blessed place, but not my appointed place. I had the job that afforded me the opportunity to get what I needed and what I thought I wanted. I misused these opportunities, and without God's purpose I did not weigh out obedient options. This disobedience would later send me spiraling out of control and ending up over my head in my spending. I was so overtaken with my new classy image that I paid no attention to what I was neglecting.

There was a far greater journey ahead for me. It was much too early to get complacent at one of life's early stops. It was just a brief time to stretch my legs for the long ride ahead. A stretch is much needed to maintain focus. We have all been destined to journey this life. It's how we choose to travel. Non-stop change will wear you down quicker than it should. So, take time to pull over and refresh your mind, body, and soul. Take time to fast, pray, and seek each step and direction for your life. Where do I go from here, and how do I get there? Will God lead me, or will I go alone?

CHAPTER 6

The Love of My Life

Destiny was in my best interest as the young man who would ultimately become my true love and soulmate actually walked down our sidewalk and into my house. Our mother eventually joined the same church Vernon's family attended.

Let me flashback to the season of my life before this. My family lived in the projects. My family consisted of my mom, stepdad, my oldest brother, and me. There was also my younger brother, Dwyane, who did not live with us. During summer and at various intervals, he would come and stay with us.

My mom connected with some Christian ladies in the neighborhood, and they would host Bible study and prayer meetings in the various homes. On this particular occasion, the meeting was to be at our house.

Having fun with my friends outside, I convinced Madea to let me stay outside and play until prayer meeting was over, and she did.

As the ladies begin to arrive, I noticed this boy walking his mom to prayer meeting at my house. He was a cute guy wearing a jean jacket that matched his jeans. Fashionably, along with his physique, he was quite handsome to me.

To my amazement, he went inside my house, with his mom, to the prayer meeting. Right then and there, I vowed I would go with my mom to the next prayer meeting. The very next prayer meeting was at his parents' house. My mom soon joined the same church his family attended, and we would see Vernon. He was always with his brother David, who served as our line of communication.

We each answered the usual "Do you like me?" note, which started our journey of growing in our newfound love. We had the usual young courtship problems, and we endured the cycle of breaking up and making up again. Then there were the in-between times when other interests would briefly dominate.

This continued until we matured enough to acknowledge our love for each other. Proverbs 3:16 KJV, "In all thy ways acknowledge Him and He shall direct thy path."

My mom planned an engagement party for us at the church. It was a time for our family and friends to celebrate with us, in this incredibly happy season of our lives. God blessed me to complete two years of college and a year on my job. We married June 25, 1971.

Here we are three children, six granddaughters, one great granddaughter, and fifty years later, still possessing the love God blessed us with.

My husband is resolute and determined to excel in each ambition that presented itself. He was unique and displayed a spiritual wisdom. He was consistent in balancing and planning for the future. Mrs. Linda James, being carefree and spontaneous, was just his opposite. If I purchased an outfit for me, I would buy something for him as well. After a few months of this shopping spree, he affirmed the fact that we needed limitations.

Working at the phone company I had to dress for so-called success. My friends and I would shop during our lunch hour and return to work with new shoes, purses and outfits. I knew this meant trouble in paradise. That's when I started doing what we ladies are notorious for, and that is hiding our packages. My secret location included in the closet, under the bed, and any predetermined location. Whenever I did wear my new attire, I would get that famous question, "When did you get that?" followed by the next question, "Is it new?" There were times I did not answer, on grounds not to incriminate myself.

CHAPTER 7

Our Family

Following two years of marriage, we had our first child, a son. There was so much active movement during this pregnancy, we nicknamed our son "Tiger" even before he was born. We should be prayerful and careful, even in something as simple as a nickname.

Tiger was almost eight pounds at birth. Hearing him crying and smacking his lips, an instant bonding occurred. Although in great pain, I wanted to cuddle and love on my son.

Four years later, our daughter Verlondra was born. Her daddy immediately referred to her as "Angel," and she was just that, an angel. Little did we know the great impact she would have on our family. Again, God knows the plans he has for us: a plan of hope and an expected end.

Another four years and we welcomed our second son, Reuben. Reuben was a spirited and always happy child. Like his big brother, he was also a handful.

We are proud parents and dearly love our children. They continuously display unconditional love and strength to our family.

Verlondra and Reuben remain a vital part of the Johnson Street Church family as well as Fort Worth Save Our Children.

Reuben is married to Lamega, and they are parents to three

beautiful daughters, Morgan, Addison, and Rhilee. He is an elder in the church, minister of music and psalmist. He has a singing group, Chosen. God has great blessings in store for this group. Verlondra is one of the church financiers and sings in the choir. God has blessed her to do so even through her shyness as she sings. She and Reuben also sing as brother and sister. The two of them often prelude their father with singing before his messages.

Verlondra and Reuben have carried our loads of life many times. They have been right there for us. All the glory and praise belong to God for blessing our children to be such great assets to the ministry.

My children give unconditionally of themselves to the church, school, and home. By home, I am referring to their love and commitment to our granddaughter Briana. Verlondra cares for Briana as though she is her mother, instead of her aunt. At this point in my writing, it is my honor to share our lives with Briana. She was diagnosed in infancy with cerebral palsy. There were medical issues involved that would change our very lives. Briana would require 24/7 caregiving to sustain her very life. The doctors told us we were in for the long haul necessary for her quality of life. This undertaking was without hesitation, because we loved our Briana. We have experienced this long haul with God ever in control of masterminding our entire journey. Again, I thank God for our children who help save us in many, many ways. We are the village it took for Briana. The village of love from the heart made it happen in the life of our angel, Briana.

CHAPTER 8

Briana
Looking at the Miracle

Briana was born June 7, 1994. Little did we know that life was about to take an unexpected and unimaginable turn. This turn would change our lives in many ways and knit us together with an endearing bond of love. God provided us the master plan because he knew the road ahead. With this assurance, we embraced the journey of life and love with Briana.

We found ourselves on this roller coaster of life and love for Briana. We had no idea of the short time Tiger had to share in the lives of his daughters Briana, Taylor, and Halle. We experienced love, joy, and pain beyond our comprehension.

Only our connection with God could see us through this inconceivable turn of events. We were entirely unaware of the impact Briana would have on our lives, her grandparents, aunt, and uncle. But we were confident that the God we serve would prepare and equip us for this next phase of the journey.

I heard we had a granddaughter, not from my son initially but from a friend that knew firsthand of the situation.

I asked Tiger if he had something to tell us. His response was he did, but he knew someone else had already told us about his daughter, our granddaughter. He felt we were disappointed because the news came from someone else and not from him. As I began to question him about our grandchild, he assured us he would bring her so we could meet the new addition to our family. Keeping his word, he brought Briana to the school so we could meet our first grand-daughter.

One evening while at work at Save Our Children, my son showed up with this beautiful bundle of baby girl. For me, it was love at first sight of my first grandchild. My husband was not as dramatic as I was. He did not express in the same way. His firstborn son was now a father, and his father was not aware or prepared to absorb the information as I was. There were heartfelt emotions and realizations my husband had to come to grips with. This news of his firstborn son, now an unwed father, took a while for my husband to process. This was not what we had taught our children.

As time progressed, love conquered all, and we experienced the blessing of our role as grandparents. Reuben and Verlondra loved their brother and therefore experienced a great love for their first niece.

None of us were prepared for the next phase of our journey. As I have previously stated, Briana was already born, and as time progressed, we realized the great depth of our love needed to sustain Briana in her fragile and delicate life.

Thus began another journey. As we begin to spend more and more time with Briana, we began to notice little differences about her. Things that were not as typical and normal. We had raised our children, so we knew there were differences in how she reacted. For example, she would stare at lights in particular and not blink for longs moments. Even if you tried to turn her away, she would still try and maintain that stare at the lights. Then I noticed how her little arms would stay in a pulled in position and it was difficult keeping them down. There were other things that caused concern, but she was so beautiful and precious that we took it as normal for her. Briana had thick, beautiful, curly black hair. She was a full, plump, and beautiful baby girl. We loved her so very much and are forever thankful for the grace of God that afforded us the blessing of caring for her. Briana made a great impact on us as to what real love is all about. As the scripture says in 1 Corinthians 13:13, and now these three remain: faith, hope, and love but the greatest of these is love.

As we became more involved in her life, Briana's mother let us spend more and more time with her, even overnight. Her mother did love and take care of her. She was always clean, hair combed, and dressed like a beautiful baby doll. As Briana got older, we realized Briana would need us in a very real way.

Briana began to have medical issues early on. Early intervention became a necessary precaution for her quality of life. This was a life-threatening situation, and something needed to be done. The medical term is aspirating, and this was a real issue in her quality of life.

Briana's mom was young, and this was her first child. I believed she loved Briana very much, but just didn't know how to handle the special needs of her child.

The doctors suggested to Briana's mom the need to insert a feeding tube to ensure proper nourishment. They gave her what is called a G-button so she could be fed through the stomach. I, with my non-medical knowledge, thought this was for the terminally ill. Little did I know this was also a somewhat common occurrence in children.

Briana could still be fed by mouth, but liquids needed to go through the G-tube. Briana's complications continued. Along with this were other complications in her life. She had respiratory problems, and even breathing became a chore. She aspirated often and would at times even stop breathing. Then there was the problem with muscle tone. Her muscles were tight and contracted to the point where she had to have occupational and physical therapy. The speech therapy was because of the swallowing dysfunction.

With all this going on in her life, Briana was diagnosed with cerebral palsy, which is a disorder caused by brain damage. Briana needed our loving support as her journey begin to unfold. Willingly, I accompanied her mom on various doctor appointments, just the three of us. This first-time mom, being young and single, was about to experience life on this totally uncharted path.

This phase of the journey included joy and pain. A time of help and a time of helplessness. A time to give and a time to take. A time of sickness and a time of health. A time to pray and pray and pray again. A time of questions without answers. A time of answers, not knowing what the questions should be.

One day I received a call that because of this situation being too much, Briana could no longer remain with her mom. There were two options for her to consider and choose. Briana would either be placed in foster care, or come live with us. The decision was her mother's to make. I am so thankful her mom did choose for her to live with us. She knew we loved Briana, and we were her family. We knew what it is like for Briana and what it takes to care for her. I know the mother's pain was deep: to have to part with her baby. It was too overwhelming at this time in both of their lives.

Briana was fourteen months old when she came to live with us. We were now embracing the long haul, not knowing what was destined ahead for us. This move affected my family in a way that changed our normalcy. This adjustment was permanent. Briana was now our responsibility, and we are thankful for the opportunity to care for her. We are faithfully committed to our Briana.

Included each time we pray at school is the request to bless Briana to walk and talk.

This brings us to another turn in the journey of *How to Really Save Our Children*.

Let's fast forward. Life with Briana was an incredible journey. Some of the issues she endured, medically speaking, included having her adenoids removed, surgery to place a rod in her back to support her spine, twenty-one days in ICU—her very life has included many miraculous recoveries. Each medical intervention was intended to give her the best quality of life. This would also help us to be able to best care for her. This phase of the journey was connecting Briana to her greater purpose.

For over twenty-five years, Briana did not physically walk or talk. Seizure activity on the brain continued but was controlled by medication, and she is still seen by her specialist physicians annually. One remarkable occurrence is she has been seen by the same pulmonologist and orthopedic specialist all of her life. Our family bond with these two doctors and their nurses tied a bow of hope in caring for Briana. I will forever be grateful for these two exceptional doctors and their nurses. They inspired us in ways we will cherish. They were there for us when we just did not understand what the long haul was all about.

Briana is surrounded by love from her family, church, and our school, Fort Worth Save Our Children. What an amazing testimony of how to really save our children. It's called love. Because of love, we persevered against all odds. With love, we kept doing what we had to do. It was not easy, but it was worth it. When she shares a smile, and stares at you with those big beautiful eyes, we give thanks with grateful hearts. It is an honor and privilege to love her and be loved by her.

There have been many medical complications she has gone through. One time she spent twenty-one days in ICU, and God delivered her on day twenty-one. It is a miracle that I have shared over and over again.

Bri had been on a ventilator for many days in the children's hospital ICU. After an over-extended time on the ventilator came the time to take her off. The time had come to see if Briana could breathe on her on; if not, I had to make the decision to allow the doctors to do a tracheostomy on her.

How To Really Save Our Children

A tracheostomy would be done because Briana's airway was compromised. The doctors wanted to, if needed, cut a hole in her neck below the vocal cords to insert a tube. This procedure would allow air to enter her lungs. It would bypass the mouth, nose, and throat. Caring for a trach was another complication in her delicate life. I did not want this added suffering for Briana or our family. Briana had gone through such a traumatic ordeal already. I had to make the prayerful decision not to do this and trust God that she would breathe without it.

Those first few moments seemed like forever; the doctors were saying to trach her, and I was saying no. In the midst of this confusion, in walks a man and joins the conversation in progress. He wanted to confirm that Briana used a breathing machine at home. He asked in an angelic voice, with a foreign accent, "Does the baby have a breathing machine? Put the baby on a breathing machine." I was ready to rush home and get it, but they had them already available in the hospital. Briana was put on the "BPAP," and the rest is the reason I call this a miracle. First of all, I had never seen this particular person during the entire time we were in the ICU. I will always say he was an angel who came at the right time with the exact message needed for this stage of Briana's life. I say this because I looked for him but never saw him again at the hospital. I just know God dispatched this angel for such a time that it was needed. I clearly remember how handsome he was and the distinction of his accent. It was how I imagined such an angel as this would sound. Following this encounter, Briana was dismissed the next day or so to go home. Oh, the joy that our family experienced as a result of this awesome moment in the life of our Briana. The words of the song, "Great is Thy Faithfulness," has proven to be true and inspiring:

"Great is thy Faithfulness, O God my father, there is no shadow of turning with thee. Thou changest not, thy compassions they fail not. As thou hast been, thou forever will be. Morning by morning new mercies I see. All I have needed thy hand has provided. Great is thy faithfulness, Lord, unto me." This song stands as praise and worship to God for what took place in this stage of the journey of *How to Really Save Our Children*.

Briana is still using the machine to ensure her breathing throughout the night. She still has respiratory problems, but in spite of that, God keeps on blessing her over and over again. She is a delight and a blessing to all who know her. She loves for people to laugh, sing, clap, and pray. It excites her and fills her with joy. It's as if Briana believes we were created to make her happy. We do our utmost to do just that. Making Briana happy is our pleasure as well. When Briana cries, everybody comes running, just to be of comfort to her. All you need to do is laugh, sing, clap, and pray, and her smile is back and her tears are gone.

At home, Briana has her own bedroom with the necessities available. Children's nursing care at night was available for many years. There have been many times nurses were provided to assist her overnight. At the writing of this, there was no nursing care provided in the home. My children and I served as her attendants. As stated, Briana cannot do anything for herself.

We have to do everything for her. She no longer received nursing, but she qualifies for the love of her family, who would have it no other way. Again I say, it's personal.

The task of turning her over to get in the best position for a good night's sleep has to be done by us. If she is in any discomfort whatsoever, we attend to making it comfortable for her. We adhere to her being on a feeding schedule to make sure she takes in the nutrients needed. This is done by bolus feeding through a tube. The family take turns attending her throughout the night. If she is sick, that is less rest for our household. Someone needs to constantly be with her. Twenty-four/seven, is a consistent requirement for Briana.

"How to really save our children" takes on a deeper meaning. It's making it personal and giving of yourself.

Because of God, our sustainer, we keep on. Because of our

love for Briana, we do it all in love. She loves and needs us, we love and need her. The lessons we have learned through caring for her has taught us to bring to life the fruit of the spirit found in the Bible. The book of Galatians teaches us nine attributes of a person or community living in accord with the Holy Spirit: but the fruit of the spirit is love, joy peace, longsuffering, gentleness, goodness, faith, meekness, temperance, against such there is no law.

CHAPTER 9

How Do You Do What You Do

Verlondra wrote an interdisciplinary research paper while at college at University of Texas in Arlington. This was one of her course requirements. She chose to research and write her paper on "The Effects on a Family Raising a Child with Cerebral Palsy." Her introductory letter to my husband and me was quite compelling. It made me that much more aware of how great the depths of love is and the distance it will travel for someone because you care so much. In essence, you allow them to live through you and what you do for them. It reminded me of the sacrifices of love and how deep and wide it can penetrate your heart. This was a true work of a love, deserving to be researched and published as a reminder of what life really consist of. If we can respond to the compassions of our hearts, the world would be the better for it.

Verlondra shared with us the research of her topic. It gave me an opportunity to really think about what effect the long haul would have not just on me, but on our family, and even more than that the quality of life for Briana. It was an honor to love and be loved by Briana. This ripple effect of love has been one of the greatest joys of our lives. It was not easy, but it was worth every smile and every hug. It was worth being there for her, because that's why and how we do what we do.

A letter from Verlondra introducing her research paper:

August 3, 2007

Mr. and Mrs. James,

I am Verlondra L. James, an undergraduate senior at the University of Texas in Arlington.

I will be graduating in August 2007, and will be getting my degree in interdisciplinary studies. I am now taking my final class for my degree requirements here at the university. This is the capstone class. This class serves as the culminating class project. In this class each student is required to write a research paper over a subject of interest to them and would help them in some way in the future.

This was a potential opportunity for her to work on and explore the effects of what our family would undertake because of our love for Briana, our grandchild, and Verlondra's niece, the child of her oldest brother—her brother, whose life was tragically taken.

I chose to write my paper on the effects of raising a child with cerebral palsy can have on a family. I chose you, Mr. and Mrs. James, as the recipients of my research paper because you are currently in this situation. By both of you raising a granddaughter with cerebral palsy, I felt this would be both informative and interesting for you and your family. This would also be of benefit because it describes the feelings that families experience psychologically, both mentally and emotionally. It also explains what the family experiences socially and financially. I believe that you will enjoy this paper and gain more insight on cerebral palsy. Finally, this paper is meant to honor people such as yourselves who is raising a special needs child. Thank you in advance for receiving my research paper.

Verlondra went into great detail on this research paper. She did a masterful job and put in much work and time.

I love and appreciate her choice of topic and honoring us in this fashion. We need each other in so many ways.

CHAPTER 10

Hearing the Echoes

As I continue navigating through life's journey, the echoes of what I need on this journey begin illuminating and bringing to life the task set before me. Time has not waited or stood still for me, but I definitely won't allow it to pass me by.

Since acquiring this hunger to be a positive influence on our children, the struggle and impact of it has seem to overcome me, and reality has hit hard. The desire to stay focused through prayer and heartfelt inspiration has challenged me to complete the work and prepare for my legacy.

The realization that there is purpose in each of our lives, and what we do to fulfill that purpose, is most relevant to our success. By success I mean happiness in knowing that I did what I was destined to do. I ask God to continue to direct my path.

Knowing that my journey involved a team effort was essential and indispensable. This team consists of those who share in their appointed time—sharing in the dream of accomplishing what I am destined to do. What God unfolds on the inside of us makes the difference. We have access to God, and there is nothing that can prevent us from acquiring our dream. With God, we are never too lost, never too far away, never too detached to hear the voice of God and receive the promises of God. My purpose spoke to me early in life. As far back as I can remember, I felt I had a destiny to fulfill. Somehow, I knew it was going to relate to children in a very real way. Even when playing with my friends, I had to be the leader and set the stage as to what we played and how we played it. I would make up rules that pertained to my advantage. If I was in my comfort zone, I could and would make sure my voice was heard. I believe the term for this type of action is "bossy." That's it, I was bossy. Now this is only if I was in familiar spaces where I was confident and comfortable. If I felt uncomfortable or unsure, I would remain the silent type.

CHAPTER 11

The Heartbreaking Challenges

A heartbreaking challenge that I often faced concerned my love for family and friends who faced challenges out of their control and my inability to step up to their pain and circumstances. My brother was concerned about our mom staying alone in her apartment in the late stages of her life. She needed someone with her at all times.

Life is to be cherished and held dear. By this I mean there comes a time in life called aging that takes on an entirely different concept of what changes will eventually occur in all of our lives. How do we come to grips with each of these phases of life is what I refer to it as the aging process. Things you used to do effortlessly now become a task. Your abilities are diminishing, and you have to adjust. A different mindset has taken control of the aging body. This change is not only physical but mental as well. I assume this as one of many interpretations of aging. We say they are getting older and unable to do those things that were once so easy to do. I say this because of what I have encountered watching ourselves and our loved ones age. My heart of love yearns to do what I can while I can.

There is no frowning upon the aging here, but a desire to

accomplish simple things to show them respect and compassion. You look at each situation as it is and fill in any missing pieces that you can. I realize there is a power within me to do the simple things that mount up to real hope and encouragement in my own life.

It is fascinating to see the compassion for one another still exist in the elderly. My mom is in a nursing facility. I visit her as the residents sit in the cafeteria. I observe them eating their food and encouraging fellow residents to eat their food also. It's as if they know each meal is important for their well- being. My mother says she eats all her food, not just because she likes it but because she needs it. She let me know that she eats for strength, and if she doesn't eat, she won't be strong and healthy. But at times she may refuse to eat because she is upset for whatever reason.

There is apparently a process to aging. You slowly begin to see changes. I know who my mother is, but I also see these changes. It is so evident that God is yet compassionate and caring in all phases of our lives. I may not desire to see this unfolding because its diminishing time itself. There is yet power in life and its purpose as we reach each turning point. Our steps serve as great contributions to our purpose in life. In the midst of aging, God still loves us. We can be assured that God is relentless in pulling us through any brokenness in our lives. God is with us though the process of aging and seeing our loved ones age. I lean on the assurance that his grace is sufficient. The love of God and our love for God fashions us into something more glorious than we can ever phantom. Mark 9:24 says, and straightway the father of the child cried out, and said with tears, Lord, I believe; I choose to shine through this process and embrace the strength of the Lord that is sustaining on this journey of life. My true identity is in Him and His love for me. This is my covering in heartbreaking challenges that God loves me and enables me to triumph. It is my desire to continue in His love in every aspect of my life. I am ready to adore and worship God and allow His power to keep me rooted and established.

Thank God for a mother who loves the Lord; I am thankful for all her teaching and godly example. I am giving tribute to my mother because she encouraged me to always be my best, always look my best, and know that God was my power source in all life's challenges. I took so much of her teaching to heart. She could make a shack look like a castle, and then add flowers.

CHAPTER 12

Life Happens for Us All

Again, life happens, and now I fast forward. Mom is ninety-plus years old. This season of her life consists of being cared for. There are signs of decline as Mom ages. I use "decline" as the term associated with the mental and physical decline in the elderly. This includes but is not limited to memory and other motor skills that affects one's ability to perform everyday activities. I am not being an expert in this diagnosis, just coming straight from the heart about changes I see. These various changes come to all of us. My mom no longer lives on her own, but in a nursing-care facility. This is not something you plan for yourself or your parents, but it is a part of life. It is a constant reminder of the changes we all must go through in the aging process. I often remind myself to be thankful for the precious moments we can share with one another. As I reminisce on life, I find myself experiencing change firsthand. This realization alone hits the target of your very heart. It can be that conversation you don't want to have, but it too is a part of life.

These matters of life and legacy make us realize we have made it together through many dark hours of life. Keeping our family together sustained us in those difficult days of life.

CHAPTER 13

Take Me Back Down Memory Lane

There was a time in my childhood when I lived with my aunt in the country. My mom was in another city, improving her skills for our livelihood. I stayed with my aunt long enough to get really attached to her. She had become a mother figure in my life. It was difficult to say goodbye and leave for the city with my mother when she returned to get me. It took a little convincing to get me to leave for the city.

However, it all worked out, and this little country girl was ready to live in the city again. City life was very different for me. The way we lived and where we lived was a community so unlike the country. Instead of the dirt roads and houses next door and around the corner, we moved to the projects. Instead of running in the barnyard, chasing chickens, or getting cold well water, I was in the projects. Instead of watching my aunt and cousins get up early in the morning, eat breakfast, and prepare to go pick cotton, I was in the city, living in the projects. It consisted of rows and rows of red-brick government apartments.

My exact age I am not sure, but I remember I had to be picked up in a station wagon and taken to kindergarten or day care. I was dropped off in the evening when my mother got off work. As time progressed, my brother and I walked to the elementary school and back home. We would stop at the candy store, which was a room in the house of this elderly woman in the neighborhood, across from the projects that was turned into a store. There we would buy penny candy and pickles and big jack cookies. There was also a sucker we could buy that would have money in it. As we ate close to the end of it you could see the money. It was our prize, which was a penny, nickel or dime. How very gross was that, but we loved it.

We sometimes walked what we called the long way home. We had fun going different directions as we played on our way. I was enjoying the city life. I did not know living in the projects could be so much fun.

We would have our friends over to watch the dance rage on television. It was called "Teenage Downbeat." We would have snacks and dance along as we watched. We had so much fun. I knew that when the program went off, it was time for my mother and step dad to come home from work. I really thought I had my timing down, until one day as I was rushing my friends out the back door, only to be surprised by my mother coming to the back door, while my stepfather covered the front door. Needless to say, I was busted. I had to pay the price for entertaining my friends. The party time came to an end.

How I managed to get so many spankings, I soon understood. My popularity with my project friends had to come to an end.

My stepdad nicknamed me, "Miss Prissy," and I lived up to it. He was a great dad, and I loved him dearly. Through the marriage of him and my mother, I learned the value of family as a unit. My stepdad came from a large family of sisters and brothers. His parents lived on the south side of the city. We would catch the bus and go to their house. We always ate, visited and had fun. To me, they were picture-perfect grandparents. There was a big front porch where we played. When other cousins came to visit mama and papa, it just added to the fun. Doing all these times, I was being molded and shaped into what were to become my family values. As the evening approached and it was time to go back to our place, we would walk up to the corner, and we would ride the bus back to the projects. A car for us was a thing of the future. Sometimes, we would ride with someone with a car, but our main source of transportation was the city bus. We pretty much walked everywhere else, like school, church, the grocery store, and to our friends' houses that were within walking distance.

There was no limit to what you could see happening around that place. There were fun times and scary times in those projects.

I can still imagine my friends and me playing ball outside, or playing with our dolls and toys. I even had the very latest Chatty Kathy talking doll. Long, straight blonde hair that could be combed and styled. Being passionate about my dolls, my friends and I fantasized as parents or teachers to our dolls. Of course, my character assumed leadership, be it the mama, teacher or whatever the main role of play was. We played from sunup to sundown in the projects, but by then I knew I had better get to the house quick.

One time in particular I was having so much fun that I didn't rush in. My stepdad kept calling for me to come in—but not this time. I thought I could play a little longer, since he saw I was having a blast of a time with my friends. He called me in one more time, and I took out heading to the door. But to my embarrassed amazement, I had been locked out. The kids were laughing, and my dad drilled me on the importance of coming home when you should and not when you want to. I laughed afterward, but I learned one of many lessons on obedience. It was what you made out of life where I lived. You could be labeled with a reputation, or let everybody know your mama did not play.

CHAPTER 14

The Rainwater/Peacock Experience

I have had the experience of meeting and befriending two of the most amazing people in my life. I have so many people who have been in my life, and each one holds a great place in my heart because of who they are and how they allowed my life to be all I was purposed and destined for. Don't get me wrong. I am referring to them being encouragement for me to realize that we don't always need to know the detailed step-by-step how to fulfill one's purpose, Just be willing to move and believe in the dream, and it will happen. Provisions will be acquired each step of the way; believe in your destiny, and God will orchestrate the plan. Life manifested into success, because my determination outweighed the lack of anything I needed. And believe me, there came the point in time I needed to know the next steps to take on my journey.

I recall meeting two people because someone had told them about our school, and they came.

The school, Fort Worth Save Our Children, was begun in 1985 by my husband and me. Our vision was for children of average- or low-income families to have an opportunity to receive quality education with a solid Christian foundation.

How To Really Save Our Children

Our goal was to educate, along with encouraging the cooperation of parental involvement in the child's spiritual welfare as well as academic advancement. In other words, our concern was for the total child.

Although we started as a day care licensed for twenty-one children ages twelve months to four years, as the children began to age, the parents begin to request that we raise our grade level. Because of the success of the learning center and the limited space, we began to have a waiting list. Because of the increase, we relocated to our present location, where we had space for more children.

We rented for several months from one of our church families that owned the location.

We were seeking ways and opportunities to support our growing educational program. One day we got a visit from someone who had heard about our school and came by. We welcomed the visit, and our students did our devotional setting with our guest. They seemed to be very touched by the academic learning going on in this inner-city school. It was a predominantly Black school with students eager and excited about their learning environment. It was a one-on-one learning experience in a more personalized environment. The enthusiasm of these children made a positive impression on the visitor, Mr. Rainwater. The next order of events that took place proved them to be a friend of Save Our Children.

In this whirlwind of a friendship, Mr. Rainwater showed up one day with equipment and supplies that the school needed. They afforded us the opportunity to be part of the project called Faces of Change. Just writing about this experience for our school brings joy to my heart.

We set up class for a week downtown in the Crescent Building. They accommodated us by setting up in a large area on one of the floors. There we held classes and were visited by the many people who worked for Crescent and other companies housed in the building. It was the most amazing experience for our children to witness and be part of learning on another great level. A city bus was sent to the school each morning. We boarded for our classroom setting downtown each morning. A city bus picked us up and, after lunch and class were over, returned us to the school. It was an unforgettable experience. We rode the elevator to the Crescent floor and met many employees; we loved how the corporate world amazed and invigorated the children during this season of their educational experience. We also did our daily class curriculum and stayed on point. We had lunch and explored the many offices before returning to our school campus. The children were excited and ready to continue the following day.

Talk about a blessing—and there's more. This experience will forever remain dear to my heart. The children experienced many possibilities they could aim for in their lives. It was as if they were on top of the world, looking down into their future. This was quite the experience. Save Our Children brought them there, they saw, and they were motivated to be proud of who they were.

There was a video production of the Save Our Children campus. At the making of this video, it was as if we were all the cast of this great production titled, "How to Really Save Our Children."

There we were, in a classroom setting being filmed. I, of course, was the teacher in this particular setting. There were my students at their desks, eagerly paying attention and interacting with their teacher. The students would raise their hands in hopes of being called on to answer questions or read out loud in class. The teacher was walking around, observing each student. Students anxiously raised their hands, desiring to be called on to answer questions being asked of the teacher. They were eager young students with a hunger for learning and sharing what they had been taught.

I was the proud teacher blessed with the opportunity to be part of the molding and shaping of so many lives. Each and every day was filled with love and joy to be able to be part of the journey of saving our children, a wonderful opportunity that God placed in my heart. Here I was right in the middle of the making of a dream come true. What an awesome experience I was in the middle of living and partaking.

It was like working in your very own play area of fulfillment. Along with living this dream come adversities, pains, and hurts. As I remained focused, I came through the good, the bad, and the ugly. It's all part of the journey of saving our children.

CHAPTER 15

We Called Him Tiger

This chapter of my journey in *How to Really Save Our Children* is difficult to write, because what goes down is the deepest pain I have had to cope with. This pierces my heart and soul. This is the bad dream from which you can't wake up and realize it was only a dream. Why do I feel this deep pain? Because it is as real as it comes. Many times, I have tried to write about this and have not been able to do it. It is fresh in my mind and forever pains my heart—and not just me but my husband, my daughter Verlondra, my youngest son Reuben, and all our family, loved ones, and friends.

As I look back and think on my son Tiger, I am filled with so many questions, and the only comfort is knowing God is my refuge and my strength, a very present help. When I think too deeply and just too bad, the spirit reminds me not to go there. God assures me that we did not fail as parents, and that the choices we make in life comes with consequences. But the effectual fervent prayers of the righteous avails much.

We went through a lot and did our best to teach our children and protect them: to bring them up in a godly home, take them to church, give them a private Christian education, surround them with positivity, and let them know they are loved.

Vernon II is our first-born. At first, I could not believe I was actually going to be a mother. But it all soon set in as I began to go through all the changes in my body. The weight gain, the baby bump, the movement inside of me. Did I mention the weight gain? It was over 50 pounds. I was huge and swollen but very thankful. I was also very scared at the end. But I made it through. He was over seven pounds, big smacking lips and all. I stayed home with him for the then-traditional six weeks. When we did go back to church, he was a big old something. One of our church mothers commented that he was big and old. We were very happy first-time parents.

We were proud parents and gave him the best of everything. He was really spoiled with love.

Little did we know we would go through the most traumatic and devastating death of our firstborn son.

Early on in his life, Tiger was busy and full of life, and did I say "loved?"—I am sure it was evident to all.

Tiger was always exploring life and happiness, from crawling under cabinets and pulling things out to climbing into our bed to finding a comfy position and falling asleep in the safety of his parent's presence.

We have a heart full of memories that will always remind us of the precious gift of our first child. He was very much the image of his dad. Thankfully, we had many moments to cherish and did not just let life pass us by. The journey is so unpredictable, and you only imagine the joys ahead for your child, not even considering the many roads ahead. Once again, the journey would take turns of mountain highs and valley lows. Valleys so low I thought I was at rock bottom with no chance of ever pulling up again. Thank God that up the road there is a rest stop—a stop where you can get out, stretch and walk, just to refresh for a time—then it's back to this highway of the journey of *How to Really Save Our Children*.

The detours are the darkest part of the journey, because you don't exactly know that part of the journey. It was the detour that took Tiger off course, but it was God's love that sustained us in our darkest hour.

This is definitely the most difficult chapter I am now writing about. By this I mean I am undertaking the mending of a broken heart. I can try to mend this heartbreak, but I can never truly fix it. I can move on because of it.

As a young man, Tiger wanted to be his own man, so to speak. He wanted to do things his way. He was of age, so he developed his own journey plans, plans not outlined by his parents. We as parents wanted to cover and protect him from everything and everyone including himself. He walked his own path and did his own "thrills" in life. He walked his walk. Our steps were to keep in step alongside him through prayer and loving him always and forever. This we did and still do.

His journey included us being there with open hearts of love and extended faithfulness to the life and memory of him: our first-born, Tiger James.

Tiger fathered our first granddaughter, Briana. I have already written about this angel in our lives. What a wonderful blessing she was to not only us, but all who had the pleasure to be part of Briana's life.

As God continued his love and protection over our son, he was blessed with another very beautiful daughter and wife. They had a very elegant wedding. Life after the wedding included another beautiful daughter. I can also rejoice in the fact that there is now a great-granddaughter. In respect to their privacy, I won't elaborate too much about that part of his life, but I will say I love them all deeply, and they are still and always will be a very vital part of my journey. I am and will always be there in any way I can for them, not because I have to but because I love them and I want to. They are part of me, they are us.

CHAPTER 16

That Dreadful Night,
No Daylight in Sight

It was a Monday night, we were home, relaxing after dinner. I must remind you that this part of my journey paralyzes my very heart and soul. I am just stiff with the shock I am now sharing on this phase of my journey. Like I say, we were relaxing in Verlondra's room, watching television, when I got the phone call no mother wants to receive. The voice on the other end just said in a frantic voice, "Have you heard?" My reply was, "Heard what?"

The answer to the question is stuck in my head, and the events that follow made it all a heart-wrenching nightmare that I could not wake from. I still and will forever feel pain over this tragedy. God covers us, and I know that God is the reason we have been able to sustain this grief all these years. He held us close, and we didn't let go. We have come too far, and the journey doesn't stop now. Up the road on the right is our destination. On the right is a lifetime of reaching beyond myself to the very nature in which this journey was so entwined: this journey of good days, bad days, hills high and valleys low—but what a magnificent journey!

The reply to my question was that Tiger had been shot. Who gets a call like that? Who can handle a call like that? I know I couldn't. From that point, my life moved into a state of daze. I was just going through the motions of breathing and yet not alive. This led me to depend on the remarkable ability of the God I serve. What I couldn't do, God positioned His angels to take charge and cover for us. From the beginning, we were carried in the arms of God. Angels were dispatched in the form of family, church, friends, and condolences who made it possible to pass through this valley and this shadow of death. His goodness and His mercy did cover us.

Upon arrival to the emergency room, our son was under the name of John Doe, because there was no identification with him. This was no John Doe, this was our son, my children's brother, a husband a father, a grandson, a nephew, and a cousin. This was in no way John Doe. I tried to pull myself together to go in to him in the ER. They had bandaged him up from the gunshot wound to the head so as to make him presentable. I leaned over him crying and praying. I even asked could I talk to him and touch him.

They said he was still alive, and they were going to move him upstairs so the family could be with him.

I even remember a young lady coming in crying and asking to see him. In my state of grief, I said no, because this was our time to be with our son. To this day, I don't know who she was or her connection to my son. I could not handle anything else. I often think about that moment and who she was and how deep was her pain. Some things are better left unanswered, I assume, since I don't know to this day.

Shortly after we were gathered on the other floor, they came out and told us he had died. My world crashed, my heart broke, and the rest is now history.

My heart was broken, and my mind was devastated. The rest of this dreadful night will remain mine to hold dear to my heart.

From that point on, we were at the mercy throne of God. We needed his grace and mercy.

At this point, we went through the period of making funeral arrangements and the pain that comes with it.

I remember well how my oldest brother Marvin and his then-wife Linda was there for us. They had a van with all the luxuries that come with it. We just rode as they carried us everywhere that we needed to go to plan for final arrangements and the funeral for our son. My brother and his wife had gone through the death of her son prior, and they were really there for us.

They even took us to Tiger's then apartment to retrieve his remaining belongings. We had so much love and comfort during this hour in our lives, but this is the part I choose to write about.

I have been to many funerals for family and friends, so I knew it took a supernatural God to bring us through without a total disconnect from reality. What a journey, but most of all what a mighty God we serve. Thankfully, the Lord leads me on and through this. We were yet born to win; we just hold on. What a journey, not just for me, for everyone, as we experience the many complexities and joys of life. It's all wrapped up in this thing called life. It is what we all go through in some form or fashion. I am just amazed and inspired to make my life thankful and accountable. I wish to share my personal accountability and thankfulness to God for blessing me with such an experience and with appreciation for his abundance of love and life.

Psalms 30:5 KJV says, "for His anger endureth but a moment, in His favor is life: weeping may endure for a night, but joy cometh in the morning." No matter how many nights of weeping, there is also a morning of joy: many nights and many mornings, which is a blessed assurance of the love of God. There is light at the end of each tunnel. This light will not be overtaken by darkness. We even have the moon and stars, which in itself is a source to help us see and the hand of God to hold us close. No matter how dark the night, we still have our daylight coming. This process is over and over and over again, and that's closure enough for me. Be assured that I can journey on with this compass of life and time, both of which are in the hands of God. Let's keep going, because it is still a journey with a destiny up the road. I call it eternal life at the pearly gates.

CHAPTER 17

The Day Bri Got Her Wings: I Am Going Home to Daddy Now

Well, here it is the year 2021, over twenty years since Tiger died and almost a year since the passing of Briana. Almost a year since we were in the hospital room waiting to move her to a nursing facility that we had not even looked into. No other place was even considered for her. I had no place in mind, and I had no mind to place her in a facility—not knowing God had already planned her exit, and it was a master plan. I did not have to even consider finding a place. There was one already prepared for her, a special place not made by man's hand. God knows just how much we can bear.

We were in a room in another part of the hospital. She had stayed in the ICU beyond the allotted times, so they had to move her. In other words, she was in the stage of hospice care.

She was there in this palliative care for the weekend. We had the assignment of making arrangements for her to be moved to a nursing facility. Her time was up at the hospital. There was nothing more they could do, so she had to be dismissed after the weekend. I call this her room of passage. Or shall I say it was her room of preparation and a more personal period for us to say our good-byes and our "I love you, Bri" time before she was carried to the funeral home. All I knew was that I could not imagine her in a facility for the rest of her time with us. Remember we were there for and with Bri every day of her life. At least one of us was always with her. This was a given. It was not always an easy task, but always a task of love.

It was a Sunday, and I had gone to the hospital to sit with Bri and let Reuben and Verlondra leave. They had spent the night with Bri in that little room or holding place, waiting for dismissal after the weekend. I had no clue as to what our next step of placing her would be. God knew what was best for Bri, and that is just what God did, the best for Bri. This was heartbreakingly painful for us, but it was even more unbearable to even imagine for Bri, life without the family by her side twenty-four seven. What do you do when you have done all you can? In the words of the song, you just "stand" in that little room. As we waited for the funeral home staff to carry her lifeless body away, we were together one last time as a family of love. As a family of caring for Bri. As a family united in love, even in these final moments with our Bri.

We touched and loved on her. We cried and cried some more. We being all together was her happy place, wherever that was. Whether at home, church, school, doctor's appointment, or even hospitalizations, Bri was never alone. This was a twenty-four seven commitment to our Bri. We were there together one last time.

We did not have to plan for a move to another facility, which meant another move, another place, which was not home with us, another place she was not familiar with her caregivers. It was another place that for us meant sadness, sickness and hopelessness for her going home with her family. This situation was chilling to the core of our hearts.

This was not in her plans, so to speak. She was not going anywhere else if she couldn't go home with Granny and Granddaddy. Home was where Verlondra and Reuben could spend the night to help out with her. Home was where she was loved, and it was all personal.

Her unspoken words seemed to echo: *Take me home. Everyone I love and need is at home. No more spending night after night in a room where I didn't open my eyes, a room where I didn't and couldn't move. A room where they looked in on me during their shift. Not because they knew I would wake up, but because they knew I probably wouldn't. They knew I would not wake up and get up and start walking and talking.* To do all this, Bri needed to go home. I am speaking beyond her earthly home. It had to be resolved by her final move to that perfect home.

In answer to the many prayers of all the children at Save Our Children past and present, and all the staff who fervently shared in Bri's life past and present; to all the family, friends, and loved ones who prayed, "Bless Briana to walk and talk," I say thank you. Prayer works!

On that Sunday, March 1, 2020, Bri got her roadmap for her journey home. She reached her destiny, and she is now walking and talking. We all aspire to reach home one day in a very real way. We will all be home, together eternally. Sounds too good to be true, but it is the good truth. In the bible, John 14:2–3 New International Version reads: "My father's house has many rooms; if that were not so, would I have told you that I am going there to prepare a place for you? And if I go and prepare a place for you, I will come back and take you to be with me that you also may be where I am." That is the journey of an eternal lifetime.

In honor of Bri going home, we had a celebration of triumph; we made sure she was heavenly dressed in the purest of white, with a halo hat to signify an angel was coming home from a job well done. She had taught us all about loving through pain. She taught us how to smile because of one another. How the touch of love could sooth her pain. How the voices of God's people young and old could soothe her spirit, how the tender care of Verlondra made her rest well and smell baby fresh. How the singing of Reuben would make her move her body as if sensing and returning love. How the anointing and therapy of Granny could loosen and relax her tense body, and finally how preaching from her granddaddy could save her soul.

Briana's life is an awesome example of love in action, how love unconditional is a powerful tool.

We have all been showered with the blessing of knowing Bri and being part of her life.

Briana is one beautiful story of life with a beautiful ending to her story. She lived and she conquered in love. Love was there in her happiness, and love was comfort in her pain. Love was there all the time. Look, she's walking! Listen, she's talking!

Praises to God! Bri was loved! Loved unconditionally, Amen! Amen! And Amen!

I miss you, Bri!

CHAPTER 18

Life after Bri:
From Strength to Strength

Just how did we do it all? Here I am twenty-five years later, still on this amazing journey of life. What constitutes a journey? When does the journey start, when does the journey end? Does my journey impact anyone or anything else in life? The answer is a resounding *Yes!* Your life matters, your life does impact more than you may ever know.

Briana's life was of great impact on all who know and love her.

When Bri left us, I had to go through a process and am still processing many emotions of love.

The family cleared out her closet, cleared out her dresser drawers, rearranged her room. That did change things to help make my grief more bearable. But I am more comforted in knowing, and don't want to forget, how Bri impacted my life. I don't want to forget the many days and nights I shared with Bri. I don't want to forget holding her close and singing to her. I don't want to forget praying with and for her. I don't want to forget that last night at home with her and Morgan, Addison, and Riley. I don't want to forget how those granddaughters stood by Granny's side, telling Bri to wake up, Morgan calling 911, and then calling Reuben and Verlondra. I don't want to forget that comfort they brought to our painful situation. I don't know how else it could have turned out, but I know it did strengthen me for such a time as we endured. They were there then, and they are here now. So, the answer to how to really save our children is, let them be children ... there is strength in the children, there is love and compassion in the children. There is hope in them, there is hope in them. There is purpose in them. Our true strength is in our personal relationships, our personal growth, and our personal commitment. With this strength we can make it through tough times. Faith, hope and love, these three, but the greatest of these is love.

Again I quote the scripture found in Isaiah 40:28–31, New King James Version

28 Have you not known?
 Have you not heard?
 The everlasting God, the Lord
 The creator of the ends of the earth
 Neither faints nor is weary. His understanding
 is unsearchable
29 He gives power to the weak and to those who
 have no might he increases strength
30 Even the youth shall faint and be weary and
 the young men shall utterly fall
31 But those who wait on the Lord shall renew
 their strength
 They shall mount up with wings like eagles
 They shall run and not be weary
 They shall walk and not faint.

CHAPTER 19

So That's How You Really
Save the Children

Today is February 23, 2021. Today is another day of remembering, a memory I cherish each and every day of my life. It is Tiger's birthday. We made a trip to the cemetery as we often do, to take flowers and clean around his and Briana's graves. We also stop at the graves of Ma and Dad, my husband's parents. This is always such a sad ritual. With tears and heartfelt pain, we are compelled to visit these gravesites of our loved ones. It's mostly on birthdays or special holidays that we find ourselves visiting the cemetery. If we attend a funeral for which my husband officiates, and the burial takes place at the same cemetery, we always make a special stop by our loved ones' graves. It's like an added officiating task to stop by their gravesites.

For days leading up to Tiger's birthday, we had been snowed and iced in. Schools and many businesses were closed. Water pipes were frozen, and many homes and businesses were without water and electricity. There were many accidents on the icy roads, with pileup after pileup because of the dangerous driving conditions. It was best to stay in and stay safe.

As I look back on this time just a year earlier, conditions were quite different. It was cold outside, but our hearts were frozen solid with pain because of suffering and sickness Bri was experiencing. She had been in the ICU of the hospital since Valentine's Day. We were taking turns staying the night to be there with her and for her. We let her know we really cared and loved her, and our family was there twenty-four seven. One or more of us was right there by her bedside through it all.

Yes, it was a cold, dry, and emotionally unbearable season. Our very hearts were frozen with the pain and agony of Briana in her condition. Flash back to the cemetery on Tiger's birthday. As we pulled up to the area where we usually park and walk to the graves, I noticed three people there. It looked like they were at the location of Tiger and Bri, but Verlondra said they were not. As we proceeded to clean around the gravesite, one of the three young ladies was crying out. You could just sense her pain. It was a pain I knew all too well. Lord, what could I do? How could I be of comfort when we were at the cemetery experiencing grief just as this young lady was. I did what was in my heart, I had to minister to her for such a time as this. I somehow wanted to be some source of comfort, if only for a brief moment. Her outburst began to touch my very soul as we swept dirt and cleared the grass off the graves of Tiger and Bri. Filled with compassion for this young lady's pain, I walked over to them and began to pray. I then asked about the one who was so consumed in grief. It was her brother buried there. He had been killed. As I softly prayed with her, a calmness came, and she seemed comforted. Prayer mission accomplished. Verlondra asked me what I had said to her, because she did appear comforted. I replied that I prayed and asked God to bless and comfort her in her hour of pain and grief.

CHAPTER 20

Thank You, Lord, For All You've Done

Well, here I am on Chapter 20 of my journey in writing *How to Really Save Our Child*. This has been a great journey, and I am now complete. My destination is in sight, and I have finally accomplished this phase. I feel I have poured my heart into making this a reality. I have stopped many times along the way. I even felt I would just settle for many of the rest areas, many of which turned into years of procrastination. The thought of accomplishing and completing this task never left. Time and time again, I had to stir up the gift. Time and time again, I had to remind myself that I had a purpose and a goal to write as I had been inspired to do.

I lost the desire to write many times because I felt I was not much of an inspiration. Then I would be encouraged by conversations with various people in my life, conversations of how I inspired them just by being Sis. Linda. Just by taking time to listen to their conversations and offering encouragement to them.

My source of strength has always been helping to inspire who I could. I was not content just making it for myself. I was not content in the normal nine-to-five, even with the benefits of health and insurance.

My inspirations began to mount as I sought to be happy in what I was doing. My inspiration came when I realized I wanted to make a difference that could not be made if I stayed in a place in life that seemed meaningless. That was part of the journey, but not the destiny. I had to keep on going until I reached each resting stop. There I would refresh and continue. It did not matter what success was in the lives of others. My success was in finding and pursuing my destiny.

I believe that is what true purpose is, and the strength to pursue that purpose is what makes us keep the dream ever before us. Once you get the hunger to make your purpose a reality, you can focus on making the journey. Nothing is more fulfilling than staying the course. You realize that up the road is your destiny. Up the golden road is the obtaining of the wings of eternal life, and just beyond that you see the pearly gates and all that is beyond them. What a journey! What a journey! What a journey! *How to Really Save Our Children*!

On this journey I wanted to help the hurting and not spend my time disputing with the blessed. This was not an option for me, it was a command. It took me a minute, but I did it.

I give thanks to the Lord for allowing me to write. I thank everyone who encouraged me to write. Thank you for telling me my writing would inspire. Thank you for telling me someone else needed to hear the things that I journeyed through.

Thanks to all the children I have in some small way encouraged to be all that you were created to be. Thanks to my family and friends who believed I had something to say. I may not have mentioned you all by name, but you were there. And you too are my journey.

Thanks to husband Vernon and to my children, Vernon II, Verlondra, and Reuben who knew early on that I wanted to really save our children. The dream started with each of you, and it continues because of you. Thank you, Bri, for being the special need that made this journey one of unconditional love. Thank you, Lord, for all your blessings and all you've done for me!

I have written my journey because of faith that carried me each step of the way, because of the hope I have that God has given me to expect things to work out for the good. And then there is love, the greatest affection of all. Love is my ultimate priority that allows me to be me and do what I do. The love of God is the reason that makes life work for me. Love is definitely the greatest asset on my journey. Love keeps me moving!

Again, I ask: Have you met that someone who can make you smile at your lowest? Who can make you believe the unbelievable? One whose words pierce not only your heart, but can penetrate your soul. Someone who cares so much, loves so much, and trusts so much? That someone who is on your side, no matter what the odds. We have, and that someone is you. Again, written by my son Reuben to "Mama." What better ending to a journey filled with so much love. This love has been the fuel for my unconditional journey.

No one can insist on the choice to grieve entirely on their own terms. Instead, we should follow the word and hope in the Lord. It is something we all must encounter. Don't allow your heart to be consumed in the pain of death to the point that nothing else and nobody else matters.

The issues of the heart may allow us to become selfish and bitter. Then we won't listen to the voice of God. It's a trick of the enemy to take away our hope and trust in God. We must trust in the Lord with all our heart and lean not to our own understanding. In this hour, we must allow God to direct our paths. Without staying before the Lord in prayer, we can easily get off the path the Lord has for us.

Printed in the United States
by Baker & Taylor Publisher Services